People Are Talking about *Framing a Family*!

"*Framing A Family* is so insightful and engaging, it made me want more! Your advice on starting with ourselves was spot-on. Growing up as you did and having your daughter so young certainly gave you strength and determination. I think the activities you included are great tools to build confidence and acceptance. In this fast-paced world we live in, we must make our families number one at the top of our 'To Do' lists! In just the first two chapters, I could see what a wonderful and helpful guide your book will be for so many families. Any time we share joy with another, we make the world we all live in a better place. With all the people that live on this earth, the ripples are endless, the gift priceless! Thank you so much for letting me read your words of wisdom and love."

Creety Becker, Flourtown, PA

"I can feel the love and persistence the author puts forth. Leading by example, she embraces individual personalities and nurtures inner strengths. With such positive, continuous guidance, no child should feel there are limits to what they can do in life! This book will put in your hands tools and techniques that truly work. It also provides exercises—gifting the opportunities for that guidance with your own child."

The Garcia family

"Robin is the kind of author who makes you want to root for her. Her wonderful stories illustrate her challenges and how she has been able to turn these challenges into personal victories and inspirational nuggets of hope for other people. I am happy to recommend this book to anyone who needs encouragement, hope, and direction to take their lives to the next level, to live life to the fullest with love, empowerment, and integrity. Thank you Robin for your creative energy, helpful insights, and compassionate spirit while providing much-needed lessons."

Stacey Toupin, Life and Career Coach

"Robin is one of the most beautiful souls I know. Her determination to make the world a better place is relentless. *Framing a Family* teaches parents around the world the value of family, union, and unity. She both guides us and gives us tools and skills. The way she raises her children is a inspiration and we can all learn valuable lessons from her experiences. Robin is a hardworking, fun-loving, wise mother. I have found all of Robin's books and talks to be empowering and uplifting... aiming to help others overcome obstacles in life and love."

Mia Bredenkamp, Bultfontein, FS, South Africa

Framing a Family

Building a Foundation
To Raise Confident Children

Robin Marvel

Marvelous Spirit Press

Framing a Family: Building a Foundation to Raise Confident Children
Copyright (c) 2016 by Robin Marvel

ISBN 978-1-61599-289-8 paperback
ISBN 978-1-61599-290-4 eBook

Library of Congress Cataloging-in-Publication Data

Names: Marvel, Robin, 1979- author.
Title: Framing a family : building a foundation to raise confident children /
    Robin Marvel.
Description: Ann Arbor, MI : Loving Healing Press, [2016] | Includes
    bibliographical references and index.
Identifiers: LCCN 2016000116 | ISBN 9781615992898 (pbk. : alk. paper)
Subjects: LCSH: Parents--Conduct of life. | Parenting. | Parent and child. |
    Families.
Classification: LCC HQ755.8 .M3585 2016 | DDC 306.874--dc23
LC record available at http://lccn.loc.gov/2016000116
Distributed by Ingram Group (USA/CAN), Bertram's Books
(UK/EU).

Marvelous Spirit Press is an imprint of:

Loving Healing Press
5145 Pontiac Trail
Ann Arbor, MI 48105

www.LHPress.com
info@LHPress.com

Tollfree 888-761-6268
Fax 734-663-6861

Dedicated to Keith -

The most amazing, supportive, loving friend and husband a girl could ask for.

Dedicated to
Emillie, AnnaDella, Karly, Kamden & Rorie -
My girls.

You are the definition of love, kindness, and confidence. The joy you bring to my life is unparalleled to anything in this universe.

Contents

From The Marvel Girls (Plus One) iii

Introduction.. v

A Marvelous Family Tale vii

Chapter 1 - Architect of Your Life: Discovering Self 1
    1-1: Defining Me 3
    1-2: I Am What I Choose To Be 5
    1-3: Affirmation of Self Care 6
    1-4: Personal Checklist..6
    1-5: Priority is Me 7

Chapter 2 - Blueprint: Being the Example 9
    2-1: Setting Your Example 12
    2-2: Self Starter 12
    2-3: Family Perspective 12

Chapter 3 - Gathering The Tools – Knowledge Is Power ..15
    3-1: Beliefs 16
    3-2: Who Passed That Belief to Me? 17
    3-3: My Convictions...18
    3-4: Explore, Learn, Decide 19

Chapter 4 - Hard Hat – Personal Responsibility.............21
    3-5: Who is in charge? 25
    3-6: Moment of Compassion 28

Chapter 5 - Bridging – Forgiveness.............................31
    4-1: Bad Mood Attitude 32
    4-2: Finding Peace 33

Chapter 6 - Curb Appeal – Gratitude 35
    6-1: Finding Gratitude...36

6-2: Gratification List..37
6-3: Notes of Gratitude 37
6-4: Gratitude as a Priority..38

Chapter 7 - Landscaping – Kindness **41**
7-1: Tell Yourself "Good Job" 42
7-2: Be Nice to You 43
7-3: Every Day Everyday Acts of Kindness 44
7-4: Family Kindness List 45

Chapter 8 - Punch List **47**
8-1: Family Goals...48
8-2: Making It Happen Plan...50
8-3: Build Your Family Up! 51
8-4: Something Positive Happened Today!...................53
8-5: Where Do You Spend Your Energy? 54
8-6: Raise the Bar 55

Epilogue...**57**
Goal Worksheet...58

About the Author...**61**

Bibliography **63**

Index **65**

Journal..**67**

From The Marvel Girls (Plus One)

Since my five girls and our plus one know what it is like to be a part of our family firsthand, I thought it would be nice to share some of their thoughts on how they see our family. Our plus one is a beautiful, young lady—Michaela Hulett. She came into our life three years ago and has become a best friend, sister, and part of our family.

Emillie: In my nineteen years of being a Marvel, I've learned a lot of things. For one, we have a really cool last name that encourages a lot of bad puns. Of course, there were more important things as well (but seriously, I received plenty of "marvelous" valentines in second grade and it hasn't stopped since). I've watched my mom wander from project to project, magazines to candles to books to speaking events, and learned to never remain in a place where I no longer feel a flame. The unwavering support and kindness from my dad taught me what unconditional love was, and what trust without question could be, and has brought me to know that's the only way I want to be.

I saw my sisters pick up these traits, and ones similar, and watched as they questioned everything that didn't sit right in their heart. And on another hand, I've seen their compassion at ages they couldn't even pronounce the word. They're small, very small, but their strong will and kindness are beyond measure, and ultimately incredible. Watching all the moving parts of this family has taught me who I want to become, and the demeanor of which I want to approach life and the people in it.

AnnaDella: My mom and dad have taught me to love myself and to be kind to others. I love my family so much. I love how loving and caring everyone is.

Karly: My family is so amazing. My mom taught me to be nice to others. My family is so nice to me and I love them so much. I like that my family helps other people in need

Kamden: I love my family. Being super nice, loving ourselves, I like that we are really happy and I love when we help other people all together and just hang out all together.

Rorie: I like that we help others. I really love our family. I love everybody in our family.

Michaela Hulett: Three years ago, my perspective on life changed, thanks to Robin and her loving family. I have learned self-respect and the importance of family, being there for one another and always having a positive outlook.

Introduction

Framing A Family gives you a starting point, encouraging your family to band together and create a place of love, inspiration, and unity.

There is no wrong way to be a family. It cannot be defined by Webster or Wikipedia. It isn't about being blood-related. It is about loving one another, standing together, being real, and sharing the journey.

Being a parent is about learning. It is about growing, acceptance, and change. It is not about being perfect or living up to what society has defined family as. We develop these preconceived notions of what we think a perfect parent is and then we torture ourselves when we do not live up to those standards we created in our heads.

I am confident in telling you that the plans you make and ideas you create about how it will be or how it should be can be thrown in the wastebasket right now. Parenting and life in general are constantly changing; every individual within the family changes. You learn, you grow, you change personally as well as a whole.

As the mother of five girls, I can attest to the fact that parenting can be overwhelming, confusing, and sometimes hard. We have such a huge responsibility to our children and the rest of the world to teach values that will create decent human beings. We have to balance the urge to hover and protect while allowing and encouraging them to be true to who they are and to spread their wings and fly. We are always facing new situations and have to choose the best response that will balance that line between friend and parent. There are lessons constantly being learned, challenges to face, and the rewards when we see our children shine. Those moments when we get that glimpse of all the years of lessons coming out in their decisions.

Being a family is messy. It can be stressful; it can be sleepless; it can be overwhelming; but it is the most amazing, fantastic, rewarding thing you will ever do in life.

The aim of this book is to strengthen families; to inspire you to build the walls of your home with encouragement, empowerment, and most importantly love; to let go of expectations and embrace the hard times and the good times with an open mind, ready to learn and ready to strengthen as a unit.

In this book, you will find advice, techniques, ideas, and hands-on activities to make an impact, to add value and encouragement in your family in many ways. When put into practice, *Framing A Family* will improve your family and life in many areas. You will watch as you strengthen and your life as a whole improves ten-fold.

Each chapter provides you with inspiration and encouragement for your family unit. The activities can have an astounding effect on your life if you choose. It all depends on how you decide to use them and how intensely you want to implement them into your life. Be flexible and creative. Explore how you can get the most out of each chapter. There is no one way to be a family. Take the time to really figure out what works best for you.

A Marvelous Family Tale

The beginning of building my family was unexpected, as it is in so many situations. It also started very early, when I was sixteen. Just a child myself when I found out I would be having a baby. It was my junior year of high school when I was told "you're pregnant" by the emergency room doctor. Those words echoed through my soul, sending chills through my entire body. Instantly I replied with a "no way, not possible!" There was no way I was taking that as truth. My mom jumped up from the chair next to me as we sat in that small room, becoming even smaller by the second. She started repeating what I had said, "no way!" The doctor responded with telling me he could run the test again; he did and it was positive again.

My mind was racing. *This couldn't be. I am only sixteen.* The next two days were spent convincing myself and my mom that it was not true. I think I felt that if I ignored it enough, it would go away—not really how pregnancy works. I decided that I should come clean and on our way to the obstetrician, I finally confessed to my mom that it was possible—I might be pregnant. We arrived at the doctor office and nervously, I waited to find out what I already knew. The doctor confirmed it and told me I was very pregnant, due in three months, and the baby was a girl. It was a rollercoaster of emotions—shocked, confused, scared, really scared. *What would I do?* I was a junior in high school, had no job and now I was going to be a parent. On the way home, I told my mom that no matter what I had to do, no matter how hard I would have to work, this baby girl would not be a statistic.

My mom was nothing but loving and understanding. She never judged me, never belittled me or questioned how I could get myself into this situation. Then we had to tell my step dad. I was nervous. He responded with one word, "Cool." And that was that—my mom and step dad told me they would help me in any way they could and they followed through with that promise. Attending all my doctor appointments, Lamaze classes, and making me any food I wanted at any hour of the day and night.

I decided that since I was going to be a mom, it would be a good idea to get a job. A local restaurant hired me as a waitress right away, and as I left my interview after being hired, I felt a sense of relief and satisfaction. Working all summer I would be able to buy the baby what she needed and head back to high school in the fall for my senior year.

The summer flew by, working lots of hours, attending Lamaze classes, and preparing for the new baby. In August 1996, my mom and I went to my high school I had been attending since 7th grade to enroll me for my senior year. The counselor enrolling me was nothing short of rude and belittling, stating how I would never make it in regular high school and should attend the local alternative education school. I refused, he frowned on that, and little did I know that he would make my senior year one of stress and discomfort, presenting as many obstacles and hurdles as he could so I would drop out. Guess he did not know my strength.

I delivered my daughter on August 20, 1996, and I attended the first day of my senior year of high school on August 24, 1996. The year was full of rude teachers, school administrators, and parents. Of course their daughters were better than me because I had a baby—so that means I must be a bad influence and negative example for the school system and all those involved. Regardless of all the inconsiderateness and rudeness I worked hard, took care of a new baby, did my homework, and graduated in June 1997.

Since my first daughter was born, I have had four more daughters. The most important thing to me is to set a good example for my girls by living with self-respect, integrity, and honor. My time is spent sharing and learning with them. Some things I think I know but most things I am learning as I go. One thing for sure the most important thing I do for them, is to encourage the girls to see themselves with confidence and self-assurance, preparing them for a life of positivity, strength, and success. I will be there each step of the way; that is my promise to them.

Chapter 1 -
Architect of Your Life: Discovering Self

The confidence you have in self determines the level of
confidence your family maintains.

As a mother of five girls, I can attest to the fact that parenting can be overwhelming, confusing, and sometimes hard. We are given the ultimate responsibility—to our children and the rest of the world—to teach values that will create decent human beings. We have to balance the urge to hover and protect while allowing and encouraging them to be true to who they are and to spread their wings and fly. We are always facing new situations and have to choose the best response that will balance that line between parent and friend.

There are lessons constantly being learned, challenges to face, moments of growth, and grand reward when we see our children shine. Those golden moments when you get a glimpse of all the lessons throughout the years coming out in their decisions.

Your family is a reflection of you. The actions you take, the words you speak to yourself, and the choices you make have a direct effect on your family. It is of utmost importance to be sure of who you are in order to have a successful life and family. You can only give what you have, and if you are unsure of yourself then your outside life will reflect that.

Being confident in the person you have chosen to be will allow you to share that with your family and pass to it along to your children.

In each family, there are certain roles each person fulfills. It is similar to how a business is set up: each person having their specific job that keeps the company running smoothly. In order for a family to be successful, each person must be working, contributing, and taking care of business. If one person is not putting their best forward, then it can shake the whole system. While we are taking care of business, making sure everyone survives, we can lose sight of who we really are. This is where confidence comes into play. Every person in the family must be sure of who they are in order to give the very best of themselves.

Take a moment and ask yourself, who are you? Not the parent, the co-worker, the breadwinner—I mean the real *you* that stands in the mirror, the person you are when you are all alone.

1-1: Defining Me

- Take a piece of paper and draw a circle. Write your name in the center. Use the space around it to brainstorm about you. Write down all things that come to your mind that you believe define you. Use this as a starting point to figure out who you are.
- Grab your journal and think about who you are. Or who you want to be. Write five action steps you can start doing right now to get you to where you want to be.

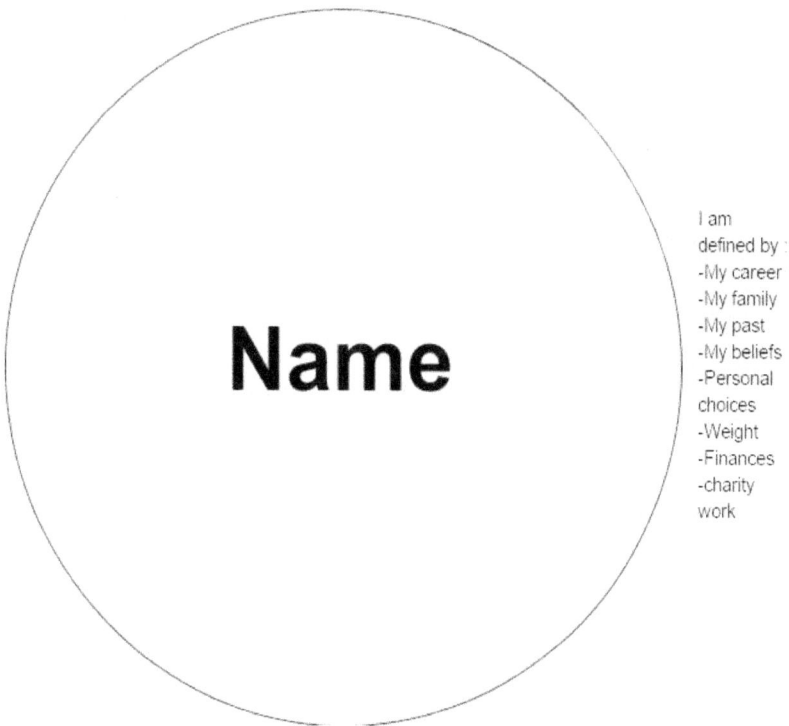

Name

I am
defined by :
-My career
-My family
-My past
-My beliefs
-Personal
choices
-Weight
-Finances
-charity
work

Doing these activities above will encourage you to start looking within and in turn building a strong, confident foundation for yourself. Your self-worth determines how you see yourself, your family and the world. If you do not see the value of yourself, you will have a hard time teaching that confidence to your children. We live in a society where it is so easy to slap on a fake smile and walk out into the world doing our day-to-day tasks completely numb. We self-medicate with alcohol, food, drugs, and whatever we can find that makes it okay to continue living the way we are, just to make it through each day. We go through the motions so well that soon we start to believe it is okay when the truth is that we are dying inside, reaching for a lifeline, hoping our kids do not see how lost we really are. Kids are very susceptible and realize who you are even if you do not. They can sense our unhappiness and that plays an important part in their lives. You cannot give them a sense of security if you are insecure and unsure of who you are.

I grew up in a very unstable, turbulent environment. There was a lot of domestic violence, homelessness, and drug abuse. As a kid, I never knew what each day would hold. Would the power be off when I got home? Would we leave in the middle of the night for a new state? Would my mom be beaten today? As you can imagine, this left me with little self-esteem. I was not surrounded by strong individuals, only those struggling each day. This affected how I saw myself. As a young girl, I started to seek out attention anywhere I could find it. In my case that meant drinking and partying, and eventually, teen pregnancy. Raising Emillie made me grow up, but I was still lacking that sense of worth. I had no idea who I was or where I wanted to go. The only thing I did know was that my child was not going to live in an unstable environment.

Unfortunately, my past experiences affected the choices I was making for her. We struggled. I was lost in life. I went through the motions like this for many years until I realized I needed to start loving myself. If I ever wanted to be a good example and give my daughter what she needed, I had to discover it within. I started to look at myself in the mirror, learn to love myself and share that with my child. The first thing I did was tape the words "I love you" on the bathroom mirror. I would stand there and say those three words to myself. At first I was negative and found a million reasons why I shouldn't love who I was. I would have to stop myself from the self-hate and replace those negatives with positives. I slowly began to reprogram my thoughts, to forgive myself and to take responsibility for my life right now. It wasn't easy, but it was so worth it. By finding myself I was able to start instilling a sense of self-love and self-respect into my children.

1-2: I Am What I Choose To Be

Today *you* start. You decide who you want to be, the example you want to set for your family. Taking the time to honor your truth, loving who you are will give permission to all the people in your life to do the same.

- Take a moment right now and go stand in front of the mirror. Look at yourself and say the words
  "I Am_____".
  Listen to your inner voice, pay attention to what you are saying to yourself.

How you take care of yourself is so important. Taking physical and mental care of yourself goes along with loving yourself.

I haven't ever been the type to take time for myself. Ever since I was old enough to help others, that is what I have done. I am kind of a fixer—I see a problem, unhappy person, anyone in need, and I grab my cape and proceed to do anything I can to help—sometimes spreading myself too thin. I realized, as I learned more about myself, that my need to be a fixer had a lot to do with wanting people to like me. The more I did for others, the more they needed me, and in my head that meant they liked me. It all linked back to my self-worth. I needed to be liked in order to feel I was worth anything, which meant people pleasing—a very negative cycle to be stuck in.

I had to learn how to take care of myself. Including how to value myself and say "no," even to my husband and kids, and take a moment to rejuvenate from the inside out. At first it was hard, not just for me, but also for those people that never heard me say no before. To them it was a personal attack; it was me saying they weren't my number one priority. This was a challenge that I had to learn to overcome. Anyone who knows me knows that my girls are the most important thing and most amazing people I have ever met. When taking a few moments to reboot, it is not because I am sick of them or that I need more in my life; it is because I want to be the best for them. When you work a nine-to-five job, you leave when the day is done and you get a vacation once a year. When you are a stay-at-home mom, there are no off-times and you certainly do not get a vacation. It is work to be on all the time. It is the best kind of work, but nevertheless it is still demanding and wanting to take a few hours to unwind, to read your favorite book, to just veg out and watch *Gilmore Girls* is okay. It doesn't make you less of a person or mean that you love your family any less.

It means that in order to be the best for your family, you have to be in the best personal condition. That means taking time to do the things that you enjoy, the things that spark your soul and feed your individuality.

1-3: Affirmation of Self Care

*Post this affirmation and use when needed:

> *Yes I am a mom/dad/parent and spouse. I am also a person and I have purpose, goals, and aspirations for myself too. It is very important that I take the time to nurture myself so I can give the best to my family.*

1-4: Personal Checklist

- Make a list of the things you enjoy doing for you.
- *My list of things I do for me goes something like this:*
  - *Reading – I have a book addiction for sure.*
  - *Sitting on the riverbank in peace*
  - *Learning about the heritage of my town*
- Make a list of things you would like to be doing for you.
- *My list of things I would like to do for me:*
  - *Attend more self-improvement seminars*
  - *Take a spa day*
  - *Spend an entire day taking an adventure*
- Make a commitment to do at least one of those things on your list this month.
- *The commitment I will make this month is to schedule a day of empowerment at an upcoming self-improvement seminar*

Be prepared for the feelings of guilt, but remember that this change will add so much to every facet of your life. It will enhance you personally and as a family. The thoughts of: *am I good mom? If I take this time, how will my house survive? Will all the kids still love me? Am I giving up on my family?* Insert your programmed excuse here.

These are normal thoughts and are to be expected. For me, I know that I want to be the best possible person and an example for my family, and that means that I have to nurture myself so I can give back to them. There is no good that comes from a burnt-out parent struggling to hold it all together while falling apart inside. You become lost, your zest for life is gone, and it affects the entire family. Your patience is gone, your temper is high, and the environment is toxic for everyone. No one is happy in this situation.

Imagine for a moment a balloon, full of air. And this balloon is you: you are full of life and ready to embrace all that comes your way. As you go through life, giving and giving, forgetting to take what you need, you start to deflate. Your ambition and excitement start to fade each day as you stop taking time for your personal well-being, leaving you depressed, insecure, and unsettled.

1-5: Priority is Me

Make yourself a priority. Find something that makes you feel alive and focus on that.

- Start small and take 5 minutes a day for you. Use this time to just breathe, be still and, rejuvenate.
- Make a list of hobbies you would like to start. Start one today.

Strive to be your personal best, giving yourself the opportunity to build a strong foundation within and watching that confidence pour into your children. Encourage everyone in your family to follow suit, respecting themselves first so they can share and live, being all that they can be always.

Chapter 2 -
Blueprint: Being the Example

Your power is in your actions. Your family may not hear what you are saying but they do see what you are doing. This is where they learn.

Love Kindness Honesty helping Others

Karly marvel♡

You are the first role model your children will ever have. Your opinion means the most to them; your words and choices create their life from the moment they are born.

The statement that children do not hear what you say, but do what you do is of absolute truth. So many times I have overheard my girls talking and they are saying things that I have said to them or that I have said to others. It is a great reminder to me to be aware of what I am saying because they are listening and learning. How many families do you know where the kids behave just like their parents? I know a lot. I catch myself saying well that's so-and-so's son or daughter, they act just like their mother/father.

This is how it usually goes, because we are the first and most important role model, not just when they are infants, but at all ages. Think about when you first heard your parents' words come out of your mouth. Most of the time this happens in mid-life. See, it sticks with us! The first years of their life are spent watching what you do, hearing what you say, soaking up all that you are. Your actions set boundaries, teach kindness, help them develop their strengths and weaknesses, building a foundation.

I remember the first time I realized I was being watched by my girls. We were in a local Rite Aid and one of my daughters had a dollar. She bought a candy bar and received five cents back. I started to leave and when we got just about to the door, she stopped me and ran back to the counter and put her leftover money in the little Children's Miracle container. My heart swelled with pride. I knew in that moment that each time I had given to a cause, I was setting an example for her. I liked seeing that!

The reason we have such an influence is because your children trust you way before they trust themselves. You are their example of how a person behaves, succeeds, reacts, and treats others in this world. You are also their example in how they treat themselves. They will base this off how you treat yourself. That's a pretty tall order when you really think about it. So what kind of person do you want to share with the world? What kind of legacy do you want to leave in your children?

When my oldest daughter was around sixteen, one day we were on our way back from grocery shopping. We were talking about the steps she was taking to build a business in the music industry. As we were talking, she looked at me and said, "I have never felt like I am unable to do anything. Having no limits has always been normal to me." She continued to say that it really surprised her friends who see limits. It has also played a huge part in her confidence and personal success. I am working hard to make sure this wisdom is instilled in all four of my younger daughters too. It can make or break their future.

It was a moment that stops you in your tracks as a parent. A moment where you know that you have set a good example with your own actions and making an impact. By living my life taking risks, defying limits, I have shown my girls that they too are limitless and can accomplish anything they set out to do. Living without limits has designed my life in many ways.

The first book I wrote was *Awakening Consciousness: A Girl's Guide!* The reason I wrote this book is because I did not grow up with a positive self-image and I had no one to teach the importance of loving yourself and building a strong foundation. I decided I wanted to give my girls a book that would give them that and get them doing hands-on activities to empower their lives. I searched online for days and could not find what I was looking for. I remember the day I decided to write it. My girls were sitting at the table doing school work and I turned to them and said, "I cannot find what I am looking for so I am going to write it!" The girls all said, "Yeah, you should do it!" So I started writing it, contacted a publisher in Michigan, and he believed in it, and there you go. If I had been worried about limits, I never would have taken the risks and made my dream come true.

I am confident that when you set out to have a family, you are doing it with the best intentions. We believe that if we talk enough to our kids about being good people, it will catch on. We think that if we lay down the rules and tell them how to be, they will follow orders. You know the statement all parents have said to their offspring at one time or another, "Do what I say, not what I do." Unfortunately for you, your children will almost always do what you do before they do what you say! Kids are smart; they read between the lines and pick up on everything. **We must be the people we want our children to be.**

2-1: Setting Your Example

- What example are you setting? What language are you using when you speak to yourself?

- Take a moment to think about the words you are using on a daily basis as you speak to yourself.

- What things are you saying about yourself, about life, about others? Are they positive, hopeful, encouraging?

How you treat yourself is so important and sets a bar for your family. We cannot just be encouraging in our words to our kids; we have to be encouraging when speaking to ourselves too. For example, I see so many mothers who want their children to love who they are and love their bodies but they are constantly bashing and degrading themselves in front of their children. They have a scale in the kitchen and weigh themselves each day before they eat and sigh with disgust as they see their weight; then punish themselves in front of their kids for how they look and then disrespect themselves with harsh words in front of their friends. How can you expect your ten-year-old daughter to love her body and feel good about herself when the number one lady in her life hates herself?

2-2: Self Starter

This is why it is important to start with self. Allow your actions, words, and thoughts to represent a life of self respect, self love, integrity and confidence.

- Explore the areas wherein you are lacking confidence; start there.

- Create a list of ways you can be a positive role model in your family.

2-3: Family Perspective

A great family activity that can help you to see yourself from the perspective of the members of your family is to ask them how they see you. What words best describe you in their eyes. Allow them to be honest. Work together to build confidence as a whole.

Take advantage of the opportunity you have to set a positive, confident influence, and shape the people within your family. Be aware that you can change this at any moment. If you have been negative and hard on yourself then today is your day—your day to shift that and start being the kind of person you want your children to be. *A great rule of thumb to follow: if you would not say it to your child then do not say it to yourself.* Be the kind of person you are proud of, in love with, and excited to be around. The best part is that your family will see this change and they will want to reflect the improvement within their own lives.

Chapter 3 -
Gathering The Tools – Knowledge Is Power

We can only do what we know, the same is true for our children. The more tools we give them, the easier it will be for them to navigate this life.

The beliefs we have create the world we live in. Majority of our truths come passed down, generation to generation. This is the same for our children. Their first beliefs will be yours. In the beginning of their lives, they have no outside influences, no peer pressure, no doubts. They believe that you are the smartest, most wonderful person that lives. You could tell them the sky is green and they will believe you and carry that into their life until they learn different. The earlier we share an open mind with our family the better.

Our beliefs also define who we are; that is why we place so much value on them. We will preach them, scream them, stand by them, and fight with those who disagree with us. We ingrain these same beliefs into our family. We make it the basis for so many choices we make, places we go, people we hang out with and we choose the friends our kids have based on this as well.

3-1: Beliefs

Have you ever really looked at the things you believe in and why you believe them? Are they learned? Are they yours?

*It is easy to continue the things we know because it is what we have always known. Take a moment to look at the beliefs you follow? Where did you learn them from? Are they yours or handed down? Do you believe in them? What patterns are you willing to pass onto your family?

Whatever beliefs you have about life and how it should be, how you should live, who you are supposed to be for social acceptance, how you look at others are all being woven into the lives and minds of your family. These truths and beliefs reside deep within you and have an astounding impact on your children.

One of the best things you can teach your children is to live with an open mind and stay true to who they are; allowing our children to see the world with eyes, mind, and hearts wide open; encouraging them to be free thinkers, to not limit themselves based on what is suppose to be but to be creators. We live in an amazing time. Things are changing. What was once truth for so many is now becoming old news. We have the opportunity at our fingertips to learn new things, to explore where we have never been, to develop different ideas and new perspectives. Our children are on the brink of so many great things. It's so exciting!

I have learned and readjusted my beliefs so many times in my thirty-six years of life. The more I learn, the more I gain, and this encourages me to take a look subjectively at what I want to believe. I grew up learning certain things. I learned that life is a struggle; you are a victim of circumstance and outside events control your level of happiness. I went through a good portion of my young adult life believing this to be true.

Then one day I was sitting in my living room, after an alcohol binge the night before, looking at my daughter and realized that I did not want to live like this; that I had to learn new ways in order to live life the way I wanted. I had to decide this was not the way I wanted my story to go. I started questioning all the things I was told and learned as much as I could about personal responsibility. I started making changes. I ditched the old patterns and beliefs and decided to adopt my own way of life.

3-2: Who Passed That Belief to Me?

- Take a moment to look at your beliefs. Are they yours? Are they handed down from your parents?

- Do you actually believe them? Be confident in building your own set of beliefs. Learn what works for you.

Allow your children to make choices they believe in. Whether it is religion, career, love, or school. They deserve the respect to make those decisions, even though it may be a challenge for you.

When our kids are young, we are certain we know what is best, and in some cases, I think we probably will always think this. In reality, the beliefs we have are the best for us and we sometimes make them the bottom line. We do not give choice; we state how we see things, and that is just that. This is not fair. It may stifle their life experience. Think of how many times you have been strong in a conviction and then down the road readjusted your stance because you learned something new. I know that has happened to me many times in the past and it still happens today!

When I was around eighteen, my oldest daughter and I took a trip to California to visit relatives. I was born and raised in Sacramento. The most powerful thing that happened to me on that trip was sitting with my Aunt Sharon at her kitchen table, talking about life and what I was doing. I had it all figured out and there was no wiggle room about it. I stopped talking and she looked at me and said, "Wow, it must be amazing to be so strong in your convictions!" Back then I didn't understand what she meant. I was small-minded, had made up my mind, and that was that.

As I started to grow up and learn more about who I was, it clicked. I realized that there is no one way to be; that life is full of change, opportunity, and growth. If my mind was always closed, how would I ever become anything more than what I was? She saw that, never challenged me, just made that statement, and to this day it impacted my life. The crazy thing is that I see the same strong convictions in my daughter, Emillie. She can be so set in her ways and thinks that many issues are black and white. It's quite the moment when I see her discover that things are not so one-way and I love when she realizes that things are not so set in stone. She grows as a person and becomes open to things on a different level.

3-3: My Convictions

- Take a moment to write down some convictions you are strong in right now.

- Be open to seeing other points of view on the subject. Allow yourself the notion that things may not be only one-way.

- Revisit it in about a month and see where you stand.

That is the thing—we have to embrace our children with open minds and teach them to see life that way as well. Let them know that life is an open canvas and what they believe today may not be what they believe tomorrow.

My girls always ask me questions about the mysteries of life, ghosts, UFOs, religion, etc. and I always respond with my beliefs and tell them that it is ultimately their decision in what they believe. I want them to know that I love and accept them even if we do not see everything in life the same. I want them to develop their own set of truths and use that to grow into the people they want to be.

Encourage your family to research things, to explore all the different sides, to be open to learning. Let them be okay with their decisions on what to believe, even if it isn't yours. These kids are developing into their own life and it is important they know that it is their path; that if they disagree with you, they will still be accepted and remain a part of the family. It is also nice to have a parent that respects them enough to share their belief but also is confident enough in those truths to let them form their own.

3-4: Explore, Learn, Decide

Next time you are asked by your children about something that has many different aspects, take a moment to share all the information from all sides.

- Write the question on a piece of paper in a circle
- Write all the different facts from both sides of the issue around it.
- Allow your kids to decide for themselves which way they want to believe. Respect it.

Do not feel the need to limit them because you are stuck in your ways. Grow together, learn together, embrace all that is out there together.

Also show them how to respect the opinions and different beliefs that others have. There is no right or wrong in life, just different perspectives. The earlier they learn this, the better off they will be.

If you really think about it all conflicts, start with the *I'm right your wrong* issue. This is true in all situations no matter who it is regarding, family, friends, strangers. It becomes a power struggle to show dominance. Think about the last battle you were a part of with anyone. Why were you fighting?

I bet I can tell you, because you thought you knew what was right and they thought they knew what was right.

We explode with arrogance, chest out, king of the mountain because we are right! This is such an issue in families these days. We have been programmed and are programming our children to believe that being wrong means we are weak- that someone else has the upper hand and we will lose part of who we are if we are wrong. This starts at such a young age. It is where sibling rivalry stems from, where marriages fall apart, friendships end, and how so many families become distant. It sounds ridiculous to lose all that just to exhibit how right we are; sacrificing all happiness just to look at the other person and say "ha! I told you so. I was right"

Families depend on the ability to work together, to live as a unit, being there for one another, encouraging, empowering, strengthening each individual within the whole. If we are busy competing for who is more right, we may find ourselves right in the wrong place.

Anyway who is to decide what is right and what is wrong. Just because we are the adult in the family does not mean we know everything. We may have more experience in certain situations but that does not mean it is the ultimate way to deal with a situation. The truth of the matter is that being right and being wrong is subjective. It is not important.

What is important is knowing and allowing that we each have our own views, opinions; staying true to your convictions while allowing others to have theirs without labels and judgment of right versus wrong.

Practicing within the walls of your family the fact that every person is right in their truth frees you from this, allowing a sense of peace within your walls that will ripple out into the world. If you start really implementing this into your family living, you will see such a drastic change.

Next time an issue arises with members of your family, your spouse, or child, I suggest you use this: "*I see your viewpoint and although it differs from mine, I accept it.*" And move on with your life. Stop the argument of right or wrong and just allow. This gives space for you and for your family and puts the kibosh on so many arguments. Honor your opinion while allowing others to have theirs.

Chapter 4 -
Hard Hat – Personal Responsibility

Making the choice to stand up, own your life and take action instead of blaming the past, your parents, or circumstances allows you to be in complete control of your present and future.

MOM AND DAD ROASTING MARSHMELLOWS BY THE RIVER - RORIE MARVEL

One of the hardest things in life is to learn to take responsibility for your actions, your life and your future. Respect resides deep within self and is a virtue of personal responsibility. This is a task not to be taken lightly at any age. We live in a society where blaming someone else is common and easy to do. There is always someone who made your life harder, who didn't listen, who mistreated you—giving an excuse for why our life is like it is. You can find blame for your life now because of your childhood, the economy, your parents, etc. but it is only when you stand up and take responsibility you take control of your life.

For me, I know *life is made of choices*. We've all heard this statement at one time or another, but to me it's not just a saying—it's a way of life. I learned at a very young age that our choices determine the successes that we achieve in our lives. Living in a state of blame for the challenges you've faced will not benefit you in any way. Luckily, you have the opportunity to transform from a victim to a victor, and catapult yourself into the life you desire.

I have turned the unfortunate circumstances I experienced as a child into a method of encouraging others, aiding those in need in the pursuit of finding confidence and strength. I am one of many who have been faced with traumatic circumstances. My passion lies in reaching out to those who can relate, and encouraging them to heal from the inside out. The result? A strong, empowered person that will change the world.

My childhood was peppered with domestic, drug, emotional, and mental abuse. I have survived countless nights of watching my mom endure beatings, can recall multiple parental kidnappings, have experienced homelessness on more than one occasion, and could recount stories of the effects of drug abuse for hours. These experiences have given me the ambition I needed to move toward success by living limitlessly. I refuse to repeat the cycle.

Every night of my childhood was the same story of my parent's meeting up at a bar, an event that would result in my dad following my mom home, then provoking the fight that would carry on throughout the night. I would spend this time tucked in the corner of a closet, covered with anything I could find to avoid hearing the abuse against my mother. Following soon thereafter, a kidnapping that I knew was coming would occur. After battering my mom until she could no longer fight back, my dad would discover my location and steal me away yet again. We would then find a place where the police would not find us, and spend the remainder of the night sleeping in his car. Although I was only a second grade child, I vividly remember wondering how a person could allow the repetitive abuse that peppered my mother's life. At such a young age, I noticed the repetition in the choices that led to that same situation each night.

Eventually my mom did get the courage to leave my dad, but she continued the same cycle of abuse. She entertained many relationships that resulted in physical beatings in the front yard. I remember shoving her in ditches to prevent her from being run over by the abusive men in her life. This continued into the teen years of my life. Not only was I experiencing the physical abuse in my mother's life, I was also watching as every adult and potential role model in my life abused every drug you can imagine. It was never out of the ordinary to come home from school and see lines of coke on the table and piles of weed on the counter. Looking back, seeing them as so dependent on this drug gave me a reason to keep as far away from the substances as possible. Their abuse showed me the real results this sort of thing has on a life, and I am thankful to have seen the truth of something so destructive.

As a teenager, I was lacking the attention that so many kids need. I had no sense of self-worth or self-love. To compensate, I turned to alcohol and partying. At the time, it validated me. It made me feel that I was good enough. Little did I know that the repercussions of my decisions were right around the corner. I was sexually assaulted at one point by a male friend and chose to take part in his prosecution, something that was anything but easy in a small town that thrived on the gossip that stemmed from it. Of course, this wasn't quite enough to wake me up. The reality check *I* needed came along when I became a mother at the age of 16 (unrelated to the sexual assault). Upon learning I was having a girl, I made the decision that we would not be a statistic. I knew I would have to work hard, but the daunting task did not discourage me. I continue to work hard and ensure that this is our truth every day. It's important to me that I am always a great role model for my first daughter, as well as her four younger sisters, by living with self-respect and determination.

My story provides a beacon of light to those who feel they have arrived at the darkest corner of their lives. I am living proof that you can single-handedly turn your own life around. I took every negative situation I was dealt with in life and turned it into motivation and purpose. I made the choice to break the cycle of dysfunction I had come to know as a child and young adult by taking responsibility for all aspects of who I am.

Although we face challenges great and small, I assure you we all have the power to live the life of our dreams by freeing ourselves from painful ruts and demolishing all limitations.

I take personal responsibility for my life in the present. I do not place blame on anyone in my childhood. I look back on it and know I am a stronger person. I am often asked if I could change my childhood, would I? I am always quick to respond with a "no". If I had to go through all of that to become the person I am today, then it was worth it.

I make my choices for me and appreciate the lessons I learned from the life I lived as a child. I have learned to make my choices count and to treat myself with respect and honor, and therefore influence and encourage the people in my life to do the same for themselves.

Now I know we all have bad days. We all have those days that we wake up grumpy, irritated, and in a mood. This is true for kids too; they are people, remember. In most situations, we expect our children to never have a bad mood—never be angry, upset, or need some time for themselves. This adds a lot of pressure to their daily living. We have to let them experience life in the same ways we do, allowing them to have a bad day, to be mad, to storm off. This does not mean it is okay for children or anyone for that matter to show disrespect or be inconsiderate. It means that sometimes we need to step back and let them be in their own space to figure out what they need to figure out.

As a parent, it is important to instill a sense of responsibility in our children and hold them accountable for their moods at a young age. The sooner they realize they are in control of their attitude and actions, the sooner they will behave in a way to compliment that. Teaching them that even though they may be having a bad day or experiencing stress, they can still treat people with respect.

I have worked to implement a sense of personal responsibility into my family.

3-5: Who is in charge?

I have practiced the following exercise with all my girls. It has fantastic power and can change an entire day from stressful to fun. I have a four-year-old and ever since she was old enough to understand, I would say around age two, I started to show her how she was in control of her behaviors and attitude. When she would start to misbehave or be ornery, I would stop whatever we were doing and look her in the eyes.

I would ask her "who is in charge of your attitude?" and she responds with "me".

I would proceed with "what kind of day do you want to have? Happy or grumpy?" Of course she would respond with "happy".

Then I would tell her that this day is hers and it will play out exactly how she wants it to. Her attitude makes her day, she chooses. This really encourages them to realize the power they have and how they can control their own lives. I would say that within our family, this activity has almost a hundred percent success rate.

Next time your child is throwing a tantrum or acting out, try this and see how their entire mood will shift when they know they are in control. This also allows them the freedom of choice, empowering who they become, encouraging personal responsibility.

As our children start to get older and the teenage, young adult years start, the dynamics of our relationship change. As parents, we have to learn to let them make their own decisions, to step aside and let them learn their own lessons. This can be challenging, overwhelming, and a lot to deal with. In many situations, this creates feelings of helplessness and a degree of loss. We have always been the one taking care of their well-being and keeping them safe. As soon as we find out we are pregnant, we shift to protective mode. We prepare by buying the things they need, adjusting our diets to benefit the growing child inside us, and making the necessary changes to welcome in this new baby and adventure. We spend our days once they are born trying to instill all the values and truths that encourage and strengthen them so that when we are gone they are able to live with love and stability.

In my opinion, all the years we put into our children, all the love, all the protecting and providing doesn't just stop because they begin to grow up and claim their independence. That is why letting go can become one of the hardest things you will ever do. It can be similar to the grieving process. For many years of our lives, we have done everything centered around the children in our lives, so when they step out and leave, it hurts. It feels like betrayal in a sense, at least for me it did. I had my first daughter very young and we grew up together. I didn't do what most teenagers do. I didn't go out to the parties; I went to Pizza Hut with Emillie. I didn't stay out until four in the morning; I got up and fed my baby at four in the morning. When I found out I was having her, I was sixteen and I made the decision we would not become statistics, so when she decided she wanted to make her own choices, be her own person, and leave the house without me, I felt lost.

In August 2014, when Emillie turned 18, to say I had a hard time would be the world's largest understatement. I cried on her bedroom floor on August 19th—the day before her birthday. I started to think about how much time I had missed; I just didn't get enough time. I was so young when I had her and I had to finish high school and work. I worked so much to buy a house and give her the stability I never had. Anyway, so she turned 18 and within two months she decided she was ready for a boyfriend, which is totally healthy and normal, but for me it shook up my entire existence. She had always been my best friend, my second-in-command, the Rory to my Lorelei (*Gilmore Girls* reference) It seriously changed my life. Now she wanted to have her own space, her own relationship, her own life. That meant there would be memories made in her life without me, inside jokes, and she would inevitably replace me. It was change—like HUGE change.

I started freaking out wondering where my family was going to go and that turned into panic about how my family would never be the same and then the fears set in about her moving out and things never being the same again. I know this probably sounds like a crazy person to you but I am so devoted and in love with my kids and family, I really struggled with this. And I was right—things are not the same. We have fought, we have cried, we have grown, we have learned. It is different. She is learning as much as I am and it has changed the dynamics of our life.

With these changes my daughter has started to learn what it means to be a grown-up—not a full, official grown-up, but how to be in a relationship, how to manage her money, how to take responsibility for what direction she wants to go in her life. In many situations, I have found myself telling her that she is quick to blame others, quick to find an excuse when things are not going her way. This is a major part of life, taking responsibility for your actions, your words, and your choices. As parents we have the opportunity to teach and guide our children to stand up and own their life.

I am also guilty of this. When things are not going my way, I can sometimes find others to blame in an attempt to make myself feel better. This never works and almost instantly I see what I am doing and make the choice to take responsibility for my role in the situation.

Some people, young and old, will always be looking for a scapegoat, for something outside themselves to blame because it is the easy way out. Blaming allows the person to feel like they are doing nothing wrong, remaining a victim of circumstance and sidestepping responsibilities. Unfortunately as parents, we usually get the brunt of this. As our kids step into adulthood, they are experiencing new things, new responsibilities, and new relationships—when they have a negative experience, it is always easier to point a finger than to look in the mirror or to hold the ever-wonderful boyfriend or friend accountable. Their blame and eagerness to make you the enemy come from the hurt and fear they are having.

If you are lucky, your children feel a sense of security from you. They know that they can count on you; that you forgive them; they will always have a place to be, to fit in and that is next to you. In the same sense, they can also use that as their scapegoat. So we as parents have to find a balance. We can be that place of safety but we also have to be that place of truth. Allowing our children to continuously blame us for their life choices will enable them to continue not taking responsibility.

Sometimes when our kids find themselves angry or in a negative situation, they become agitated. This attitude pours over onto the family. They work hard to make negative actions okay by lashing out at the people who love them the most. It's easier that way, because attacking within the family, they have the knowing that we will always be there and always forgive. Also, it allows them to justify the situation, continue on and not have to face the actual issue.

I am the kind of mom who will call my nineteen-year-old daughter out and tell her she is making excuses, directing her anger toward the wrong people, and not taking responsibility. I want her to be aware so she can look at the situation and make the choice of her next step. In many instances, this can lead to more frustration for her and in turn me. I feel that if I do not stand up and make her accountable now, she may not know how to handle real life situations in the future. It is my responsibility now. If she intends to go out into the world and be productive, she has to be willing to accept this and own her life, all aspects of it. I understand she is learning and growing right now, that is why it is the perfect time to guide her toward personal responsibility.

A lot of times I will encourage her to look at the situation with a different perspective. Like, *what if your younger sister was in the same place you are right now, what would you suggest to her?* This makes her stop and think of what advice she would give and can help her to reevaluate the situation.

3-6: Moment of Compassion

If you find yourself in a similar situation—take a moment to look at your child, see the hurt, feel compassion, offer love freely, but keep them in check. Do not allow yourself to be disrespected, lied to, or blamed for where they are right now. Encourage them to respect who they are enough to behave with kindness.

Also keep in mind the importance of forgiveness. We all make mistakes and it is within the walls of our family we can teach love, patience, and forgiveness.

Forgiveness is one of the most powerful tools known to mankind. It can heal so many wounds.

Chapter 5 -
Bridging – Forgiveness

Making mistakes is a part of learning. Forgive and
appreciate the lessons learned.

One of the most powerful tools in life and in family is the ability to forgive one another. Realize that people make mistakes; we all do. No matter the age, we all say and do things that may not be nice and hurt one another. Most times unintentional, but there are always those intentional hurts too. The most powerful way to move past these situations is to take responsibility, apologize, and forgive. This will allow growth and give you the ability to be a strong family.

In many families, it is common to expect the children to always be on their best behavior—to never have a lapse in judgment and not step out of line. These are unrealistic and unfair expectations. As I mentioned earlier, kids are people just like us. They go through moods and act out and sometimes are not very nice—just like adults. The difference is that we as parents have a hard time accepting that. We have decided how they are going to act and if they do not follow that line then we can react in a negative way with punishments.

4-1: Bad Mood Attitude

- Think of the last time you punished your child because they were in a bad mood.

- Now think about the last time you were in a bad mood and how you treated yourself. We usually find some compassion for why we are behaving that way.

- Look for that same compassion for your child in that moment. It can make a huge difference in your relationship.

I am guilty of this. Years ago, before I started learning about the way I wanted to parent, I only knew what I knew. I had two daughters at this time and I did not know how to be a positive parent. If one of my girls had a bad day I only knew to get after them and punish their behavior. I never thought about them having a rough night or stressful morning. As I started to learn the kind of impact I wanted to make on their childhood, I started to ask for forgiveness for my behavior. I wanted to let them know that I am responsible for my actions and that it is okay for them to have a bad day.

Practicing forgiveness in your family will open doors, empower everyone, and change relationships. Yes, it is that powerful.

We have all been so mad before that we have said or done something that has made us feel bad later on after we calmed down. Sometimes we can be so angry we become irrational, lashing out toward the people we love. It's always easier to be mad at the people we are closest to because in the back of our minds, we know they will forgive us. When you realize that you have been hot-headed it is absolutely of utmost importance to say "I'm sorry". This includes apologizing to your children. Just because you are the parent does not give you a free pass to misuse your kids. Saying sorry allows you to set an example by taking responsibility for your actions. It enables you to release the angry, hurt emotions that go along with the situation. This way you can let go, move forward, and heal.

4-2: Finding Peace

- The next time you are angry with your family, take a moment to breathe, then sit down with the person that you are angry with; listen to their side of the story; tell them why it hurt you; work together on a solution.
- Practice this activity the next time you make your child angry too. Allow them to be honest with you and respect what they are saying. Ask for forgiveness. Learn together and diffuse the situation.

It is also a good idea to accept apologies when the people in your family are giving them out. I understand that sometimes we can be really hurt, especially when it comes from the people we love the most and trust more than anyone in the world. The thing is that, like I said earlier, we all make mistakes and the longer we hold on to the anger and hurt, the longer we suffer. The more we stay in this negative space, the harsher effect it has on our relationships and family as a whole. It can be beneficial to realize that forgiving someone else is not about the other person; it is about you. It is about setting ourselves free from the pain and carrying around the damage. We do not have to agree with the person that hurt us but we must forgive and let go so we can live a happy life.

If you find yourself in a situation where you are unable to forgive the other person then it is best to remove that person from your daily life. It does not mean you do not love them; it just means you respect yourself enough to stop allowing toxic relationships to take place in your life. Set boundaries, keep those boundaries, and move forward.

Chapter 6 -
Curb Appeal – Gratitude

A moment of gratitude shapes your attitude.

If you are looking for a way to empower, connect, and grow as a family, gratitude is the place to start. Living in a state of gratitude can and will shift the way you are living. It isn't just about being grateful for the things that you have; it is about finding appreciation for all situations, people, and the ups and downs of living. A sense of gratitude comes from within, a mindful choice which means you are able to make this a family choice, a way of life for everyone. As the alpha person in your family, you are in charge of setting the tone. Lead by example by working on yourself, removing focus from the small stuff that doesn't really matter to the real stuff of life. You know the stuff that makes it worth it—like your children laughing, feeling good about you, breathing—the things that are irreplaceable. Accept and appreciate the opportunities in seeing the brightness in all things, big and small. This shifts your mindset to positivity. As you are living with this attitude, it will trickle over and imprint your entire family.

Now I know we all can have a bad day, wake up on the wrong side of the bed with an attitude to go with it. Or we can face a combative situation with our kids getting them up and ready for school, working to get out the door, and all that stress that goes along with it. These moments are when it is imperative to take charge and find something to be grateful for. The times I am in these situations I take the time to find something that reminds me how lucky I am.

6-1: Finding Gratitude

Try this activity the next time you are forgetting how fortunate you are and I promise it will shift your mood to gratitude, if even just for a few moments.

*Look around your house and find something simple as a houseplant that brings you joy, or your new blanket, your favorite cereal in the cupboard, your favorite CD—just anything that brings you instant happiness. As you focus on the gratitude you have for this item, you will instantly raise your vibrations and shift your mood. This may take a few tries, but you will get it! So keep at it!

The reason an activity like that works is because you cannot be in a state of despair and a state of gratitude at the same time. It's impossible. Give it a try and teach this to your family so you can all participate.

6-2: Gratification List

- Create an instant gratification list for your family, writing fifteen things that instantly bring a smile to your face.

- Include things for all members of the family. Memorize them. Let them be your go to the next time you need a pick me up. Encourage your entire family to participate.

In my own experience, if I wake up with negativity, I am quick to change my state of mind by listing all the things I am grateful for, including being able to eat, to see, to breathe, and it shifts me instantly.

One of the most valuable things in life is the ability to appreciate the people in your life. Face it, we are all busy; we all have responsibilities, chores, jobs, and things that take up our twenty-four hours each day. Our family is not always at the top of that list. Most of these responsibilities we are taking care of are for the benefit of our family, but it is easy to set them aside to get stuff done. We fill our days with distractions and can lose sight of the important things in our lives. When you are part of a family, gratitude for one another is of utmost importance. It makes sure that each individual feels complete and needed. One of the greatest feelings in the world is knowing that you are appreciated and this goes for everyone no matter their age. It changes your attitude, makes you aspire to be a better person, and creates a feeling of absolute love.

6-3: Notes of Gratitude

- Sit with your family—take a moment to think of the members in your family and why you are grateful for them.

- Write each family member's name at the top of a

notecard—add a quick note for each person in your family with the reason you appreciate them.

- Pass it around to each member, so each person shares their gratitude. Give that notecard to the person listed on top. It will act as a reminder.

I understand that we get in a routine as a family, playing our roles and going through the motions, becoming preoccupied with living. Gratitude for our family can be pushed to the side. Realizing how appreciation changes the entire vibes of your family will encourage you to make this a priority in your daily living.

6-4: Gratitude as a Priority

Here are a few ideas to get you started:

1. **Tell your spouse/significant other that you appreciate the things they contribute to the family**. It can be small things or big things- It really doesn't matter just as long as you are noticing. For me I am always eager to tell my husband thank you for taking the time to listen, to hear what I am saying, and know that in that moment, I just need him to listen, encourage, and be there.

2. **Include your children**. In many families, children are just there. They are not included in the daily living, vacation planning, TV shows you watch, bill paying etc. And in some cases, they do not even know what is going on at all. Letting your kids in on the decisions being made lets them know that they are an important part of the family and their opinions and ideas are valued. I have always included my girls in everything our family does. They weigh in on decisions we are making; their opinions are listened to and appreciated. They know that we are a family, a unit and we couldn't do it without them.

3. **Make home for everybody**. Your surroundings play a very important part in your life. If you fill your home with strict rules, clutter and negativity, that will reflect in your daily living and in the daily living of our family. Let your home be free, allow the space to be for everyone—not just

your style, your things, and your likes. My house is an absolute hodgepodge of our family. I am so grateful for that. I like that my bathroom looks like a make-up, hair product explosion after we all get ready. I like that at night my husband clears a path through the toys in the living room before bed. I like that I know the theme song to every Disney and Nickelodeon show. I like that my house is never quiet, always messy, and I am always surrounded by craziness. It's all these little things that combine all the unique characteristics of each member of our family. This is home, not just my home but the home of six other people.

Appreciation makes such a difference in the happiness and energy of your family. Take the time to implement gratitude into how you treat each person. Be sure to not only say it but also show it.

Chapter 7 -
Landscaping – Kindness

Be the person that is remembered for their kindness, leaving
each person you meet a little happier.

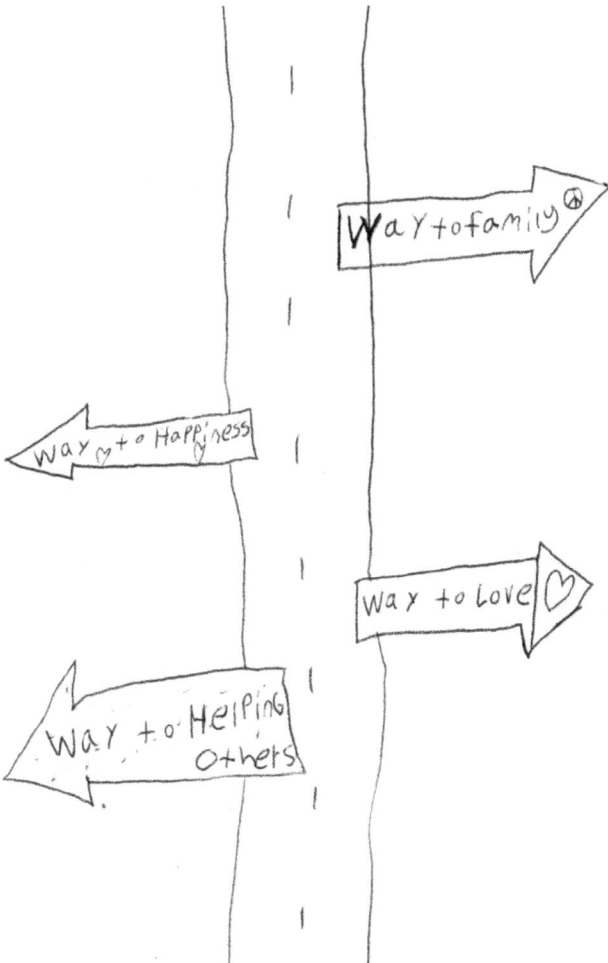

Way to family ☮

Way to Happiness ♡

Way to Love ♡

Way to Helping Others

One of the most powerful phrases we use at our house is *nice matters*. I have always been the kind of person that walks with kindness and I have been instilling this in my girls since the day they were born.

Treating others with love, compassion and kindness speaks volumes about who you are. The world can be a struggle for some people and the fact that we have the ability to step in and make life a little brighter, a little easier for someone is quite the honor. No matter how old your children are, they are old enough to learn how to be a kind person. This is going to start with the way you treat yourself. Yes you, the one they are looking to for guidance to become the kind of people that imprint this world.

The impact your have on your family is so strong, you are essentially the foundation on which the whole structure is built. You must know this and embrace it. I know that you think if you are nice to others, your kids will catch on and do as you do. That is not always the case. Children see their parents as superheroes, flawless, as the best people on Earth. They are watching you every moment hanging on to your every word, mimicking every action. It is so important to treat yourself with love and compassion, not just for your family but for you too. In many situations, it is easier to be nice to others than to ourselves. We find it unethical and rude to be critical of another person but when it comes to ourselves, we can tear us apart from one end to the other.

7-1: Tell Yourself "Good Job"

> • When was the last time you told yourself good job for a task you completed?

It is typical to be hard on yourself because we are our biggest critics. We can find fault in everything we do. Our lack of patience for growth and mistakes leads to being mean to ourselves. And sometimes this leads to being negative toward our families as well. When we are low on self-esteem, it is very easy to lash out at the people we love the most.

7-2: Be Nice to You

Here is a challenge for you the next time you are being harsh to yourself.

- Pause, step back for a moment, think of how you would treat your child in this same situation.

- Would you yell, belittle, and call names? Probably not.

Now then, why are you treating yourself this way? You deserve patience, kindness, and love too. You are worthy of that. You are learning and growing too; allow yourself that.

Think back to the people in your life that stand out. Who are they? What makes them stand out? If I had to guess, it is the ones that were kind and loving to you, the ones that pulled you up and made you feel important. The ones that gave you those moments to write home about. Be that person to your family. To me it has always been important to make sure my girls know they are loved, to show them kindness and compassion. Each night since my first daughter was born nineteen years ago, I have said, "I love you. Glad I have you." It is something that means a lot. I want each of my children to know without a doubt that their existence is appreciated.

The first person I remember treating me with kindness was my Kindergarten teacher, Mrs. Castaneda. Her classroom was a place of love and peace for me, escaping the reality of an abusive home life. She never judged me because of the lifestyle my parents lived; she showed unconditional acceptance and love. I often think of her and the impact a person can have on you. This encourages me to instill kindness, acceptance, and love in my children.

It is important to teach your children how to be the change, to be the person who reaches out in kindness, caring about helping others. We find so many people out there that build up walls because they have been taught by their parents or others to not let others in because people are mean; that the world is a cruel place full of hateful, unkind individuals. If this is what you see and what you are teaching your children, it is what you will live.

My family does a lot of work with the homeless and less fortunate. We are often surprised by the people that are scared and standoffish to those less fortunate. I have been told by many members of different communities that they are not comfortable encouraging the homeless to come into their towns. They see these people as a threat because they are different. We have to show our children that just because someone is in a rough spot doesn't mean that they do not deserve respect and kindness.

We must practice the golden rule:

Treat others the way you would like to be treated.

It reminds me of the whole issue of bullying. Everyone has either been bullied, watched someone else being bullied, or has actually bullied someone else. I am confident in saying that any form of bullying behavior starts in the home. I watch kids being very mean because someone is different; they wear dirty clothes; their family doesn't stand up to the societal expectations; they learn differently; they don't have name brand items. The list could go on forever.

The point is that although we usually associate bullying with kids, it is actually a very real problem within many families. The children watch their parents bullying each other, mistreating them, and/or lashing out at other families in the community. It comes back to feeling the need to belittle others to feel more confident within—the whole keeping up with the Joneses. As a family, you must instill a sense of self love and confidence into every inch of your family. This will eliminate the need to be mean, empowering your child within, and creating a kind, loving human. Guide them to help others and not to judge.

7-3: Every Day Everyday Acts of Kindness

Implement the practice of random acts of kindness into your family life. Actually I would rather call this Everyday Acts of Kindness, because being kind should not be a random act but a basic act that we practice every day, a normal thing. There are so many simple things you can do. Here are a few ideas:

- Open a door for a stranger.
- Let someone in while you are driving.
- Give a compliment.

- Pay for someone's coffee behind you in line.
- Rake the neighbor's leaves.

These are very simple things you can do. Doing them with your children will show them the importance and encourage them to act the same way.

I love the way my girls are on board to help anyone in need. For example, a couple weeks ago, my girls and I were driving around town on the golf cart, enjoying a summer day. We spotted a local lady cleaning her garden beds. She was an older lady and seemed to be getting tired out and was taking a break every few minutes. So we pulled up and offered to help her. The five ladies jumped off the golf cart eager to help, no complaining, no whining, just waiting for instruction. We visited with this lady and she could not believe we were there to help her. She made the comment, "This is the first time anyone has just helped me." That was so amazing to hear and know that we have impacted her life and she has ours. She was 87 years old and it was a wonderful visit. Now every time we go past her house, the girls and I have that memory of how we helped someone and made a difference.

That is the kind of people that our world needs. And how great is it that you can create this sense of kindness and compassion in your family.

7-4: Family Kindness List

- Make a list of some things you can do starting today to encourage kindness within your family.

Chapter 8 -
Punch List

Hands-On Family Activities to Encourage Action

No matter what you are doing in life, if you want to
succeed, you must take action.

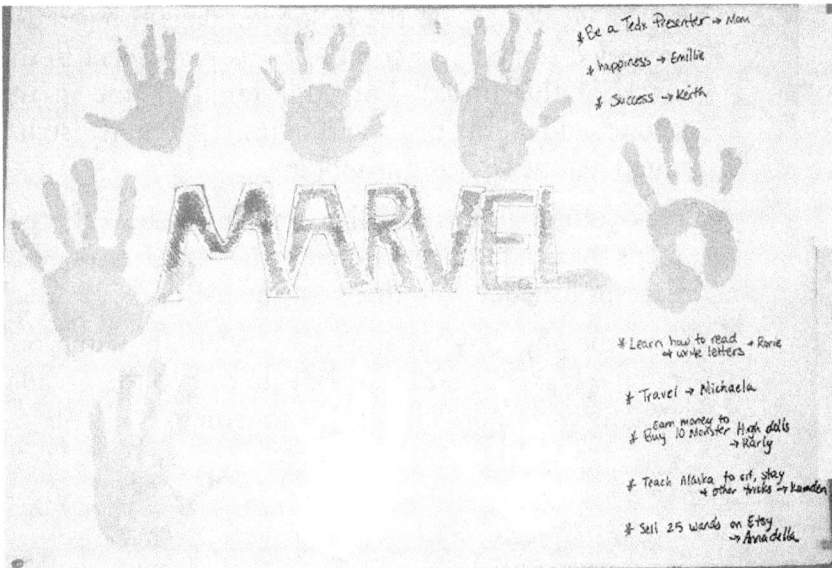

Now that you have worked together as a unit to strengthen from the inside, it is time to take action. This section of this book is about just that, taking action. I am providing you with worksheets that will encourage working together and getting back to that core family.

As an individual, you may set personal goals and work to achieve them by yourself. Goals are our roadmaps to getting from one place to another. They are your plan. What I propose is that you do some goal setting as a family, providing your family with direction and setting life in a positive motion.

Your family is your unit. Your success and well-being depend on one another. The most powerful way to get things moving in a positive direction is to create some goals, focusing your intentions toward something you all want that will benefit the entire family. Working together will only enhance your life and opportunities for success.

8-1: Family Goals

- Use the worksheet on the following page (I have also included some extra copies of this worksheet in the back of this book). Put your family name in the center, add family goals within the circle, and also list them below. Use this as guidance.

- Break your goals into smaller steps and assign different steps to each family member. As the smaller goals are accomplished, check them off the list.

- When the goal has been reached, celebrate with your family. Have a pizza party or go out to the arcade. Whatever you do, all enjoy it together.

The _____ Family Goals:

1. _____

2. _____

3. _____

4. _____

5. _____

8-2: Making It Happen Plan

In my most recent book, *Life Check: 7 Steps to Balance Your Life!*, I shared a Making It Happen Plan. I am going to share it here too with emphasis on how to implement it into your family. This can really get things moving, inspiring your family to work together toward success.

Step 1: Decide what you want as a family. This may take some time because we can all be heading in different directions. So it is really beneficial to sit down as a collective whole and decide what you all want. A great indicator that you are on the right path is when you all feel excited about the direction.

Step 2: Break your goals into steps. Assign each person in the family a different step. Taking the time to plan it out in steps will make it manageable. Your family will see the goal from an obtainable viewpoint and as each step is completed, there will be a sense of accomplishment.

Step 3: Take action. The only way anything can happen is by taking action. You can list your goals, break them into achievable steps, but if you continue to just sit on the couch, then you are guaranteed to achieve nothing. To be most effective, correlate your actions to the steps you have listed above.

Now that you guys have created an effective three-step plan to set your goals in motion, you must figure out how determined the family is to making these goals a reality.

- Start to visualize how you guys will accomplish your goal. Envision the family taking these steps. Practice this exercise each day with the family. It will slow everyone down and keep a universal focus on the goals.

- Make a list with your family of five things you can each do a day to move you closer to making your goals happen.

- Keep in mind the determination of your family will determine whether or not you goals come to life.

8-3: Build Your Family Up!

We have to build our family up, to strengthen from the inside out. We must use our voice as parents to encourage, empower, and ignite the souls of our children. I have compiled a cheat sheet for you that includes ten things every child needs to hear and why the words you are saying are so important in the success of their lives, now and in the future.

1. **I love you.** It is the obvious one. These three words have such an impact. It lets your child know they are accepted and that you appreciate their presence in your life. It develops a sense of trust, giving them courage to live fully knowing your love is there.

2. **You are worth it.** We base everything in our lives off what we think we are worth. This is true no matter what age you are. If your child never knows they are worth respect, love, and kindness, they will allow others to treat them without respect, without love, and without kindness.

3. **You can do it.** Kids cannot be discouraged by the red tape of life if they are always encouraged by you. The only limits we have are the ones we create. No matter how big or small a goal is, it is achievable. If your child knows you are supporting them, they will soar to new heights.

4. **I'm sorry, can you forgive me?** Face it we as parents make mistakes, we are human; we are growing and learning too. Asking our children for forgiveness shows respect; it shows that we value their opinion of us and we see our error and we are taking responsibility for our actions, setting an example, teaching forgiveness and responsibility.

5. **I believe in you.** As your child journeys off into the world, they will face obstacles and sometimes doubt themselves and the direction they are heading, knowing that you believe in them, that your fan enables them to stay strong in what they are doing. They can confidently go forward because you are in their corner, even if no one else is.

6. **Do not underestimate yourself.** This world is big. Opportunities are everywhere. Encourage your children to know their greatness, to embrace life with open arms and an open mind. Go out and explore all that life has to offer. The world awaits what they have to bring; make sure they know that.

7. **Thank you.** There is nothing better than knowing you are appreciated. These two little words can inspire someone to be a better person. It lets your child know that you recognize what they have done and they are appreciated for it. It also shows respect to them. A lot of times kids do chores and take care of their responsibilities without the acknowledgment of gratitude from their parents. This can make them feel like the things they are doing are not of significance. Take the time for these two words.

8. **No.** You have to be prepared to say no to your kids. Whether it is in a disciplinary situation or just something they want, it is important to be able to tell them no. It really makes the process easier when we can tell them why we are saying no. I have always been the kind of parent who explains to my kids why things are the way they are. If I tell them no, it is because I feel it is in their best interest. This creates a level of trust because they realize you are not being harsh but providing them with real facts of why you are saying no.

9. **You make a difference.** Every single person on Earth makes a difference. Just your presence has made life different. No matter if you are a scientist, a doctor, a mom, a housekeeper, for a kid, your life is important. Your choices, your actions all have changed our planet and no matter what you do, you make a difference. Now what difference you choose to make is up to you, positive or negative—that's on you.

10. **Be nice.** There are plenty of "critics" and mean people in life; be the nice one. Go out of your way to make life a little brighter and a little kinder to others. If you see someone in need, be that hand up.

8-4: Something Positive Happened Today!

Each day we have the opportunity to focus on something positive to keep us going in a great direction. This worksheet gives you a prompt for each day of the week to create focus. Do this together each day with your kids. Listen to them, let them share what they are experiencing. It really is beneficial for all because you are slowing down and sharing.

Sunday	Three great things about myself right now are…
Monday	Today I accomplished…
Tuesday	I felt good about myself when…
Wednesday	Today I am a success because…
Thursday	I honored myself today by….
Friday	Today I felt empowered when…
Saturday	Today I had a positive experience with (person, place, or thing)…

8-5: *Where Do You Spend Your Energy?*

This next worksheet is powerful and can give you the opportunity to explore and encourage your children to focus on the positive in situations, directing them to spend their energy on building something positive versus staying stuck in the negative of certain issues.

"*It's about living your truth while allowing others to live theirs.*"

What You Oppose	What You Support
Bullying	Encourage kindness by example
Animal Abuse	Help animals in need
War	Speaking up on peace

Creating a family coat-of-arms or crest ("shield") is a fun

activity that can encourage your children to take pride in the family and what you all stand for.

8-6: Raise the Bar

I use this worksheet in my workshop titled "Raise the Bar". It is all about finding inspiration, getting busy and making things happen in your life! This is great to use alongside your goal setting. Each step gives you a direction to take.

1. **Start a fire.** Find something that inspires you; that ignites your soul.
2. **Rock the boat.** Test the waters. Stand up and get things moving.
3. **Actions --> Words.** You have to quit talking and start taking actions. It is about making things happen.
4. **Tailor-made attitude.** Your attitude will determine your success. Embrace things with positivity and determination.
5. **Cha-cha forward.** As you proceed, you may hit a roadblock. This is ok. Use it as motivation to propel yourself to the next step in life. You got this!

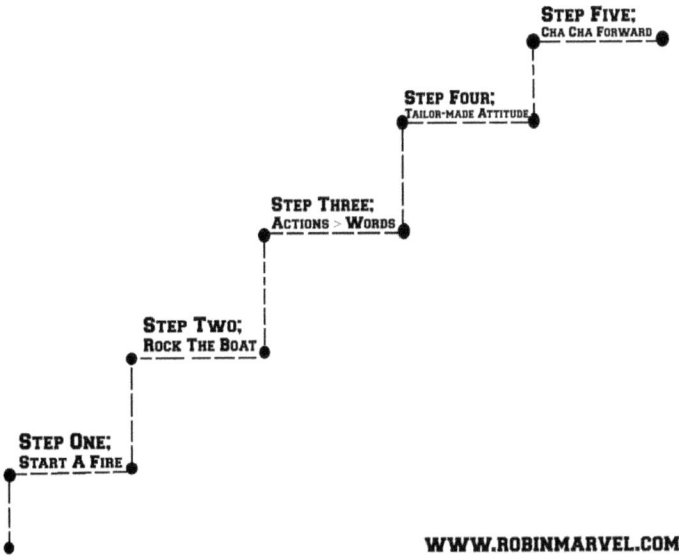

STEP FIVE:
CHA CHA FORWARD

STEP FOUR:
TAILOR-MADE ATTITUDE

STEP THREE:
ACTIONS > WORDS

STEP TWO:
ROCK THE BOAT

STEP ONE:
START A FIRE

WWW.ROBINMARVEL.COM

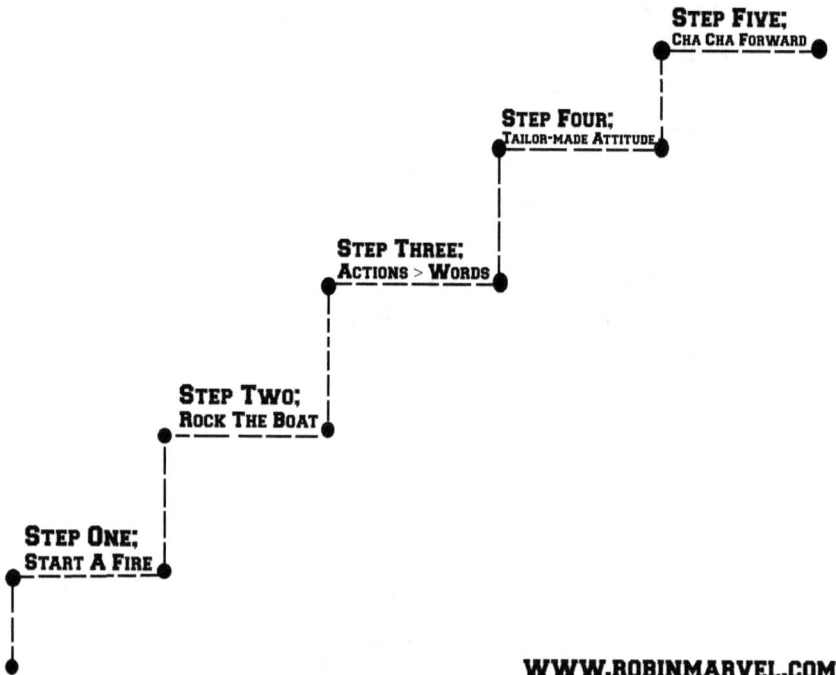

STEP FIVE:
CHA CHA FORWARD

STEP FOUR:
TAILOR-MADE ATTITUDE

STEP THREE:
ACTIONS > WORDS

STEP TWO:
ROCK THE BOAT

STEP ONE:
START A FIRE

WWW.ROBINMARVEL.COM

Epilogue

As a mom of five, I can confidently tell you that having a family is by far the greatest thing I have ever done. It is the most exciting, most trying, and the most spectacular thing I have ever experienced. I am always learning, always growing and sometimes going completely crazy!

As a mom, I always strive to be the one they can count on, the one that always keeps it real, and the one who they feel safe with. My goals are to provide a safe, happy, fun environment as they grow. So when they grow up, they look back on their life and remember the crazy mom that danced away to baby got back, the mom that always wanted them by my side, the mom that would give her heart to them in a second if they needed it. But also the mom that taught them to respect who they are, use their voice to stand in their truth, and to help anyone in need.

For me, it's always been about the love. There were many situations that I didn't understand; there still are some, and I am sure there are many to come. But no matter what the situation, I am always in my girls' corner, always cheering them on, always wanting to see them succeed, believing in them unconditionally and watching from the sidelines as they grow into who they want to be.

If I had to leave them with one lesson, it would be to respect yourself—to know your worth and never let anyone take away from that. There are many people who will try because they feel bad about themselves. You have to be strong within and walk away from people like that. It is so easy to question ourselves as we grow and learn and sometimes we can't even understand who we are or why we are where we are. As long as you are confident within, you will take those times and come out of the storm with strength, wisdom, and a love like nothing else.

You are irreplaceable, beautiful, and amazing. Always stand tall in who you are. My life and this world is a better place because of you.

Goal Worksheet

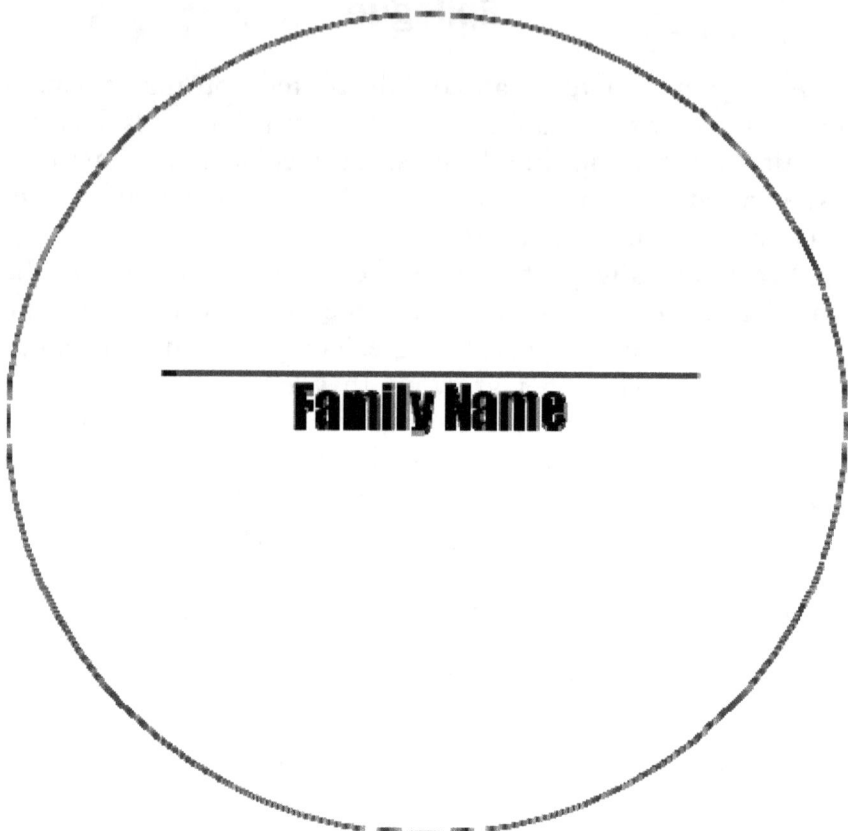

_____
Family Name

The _____ Family Goals:

1. _____

2. _____

3. _____

4. _____

5. _____

Goal Worksheet

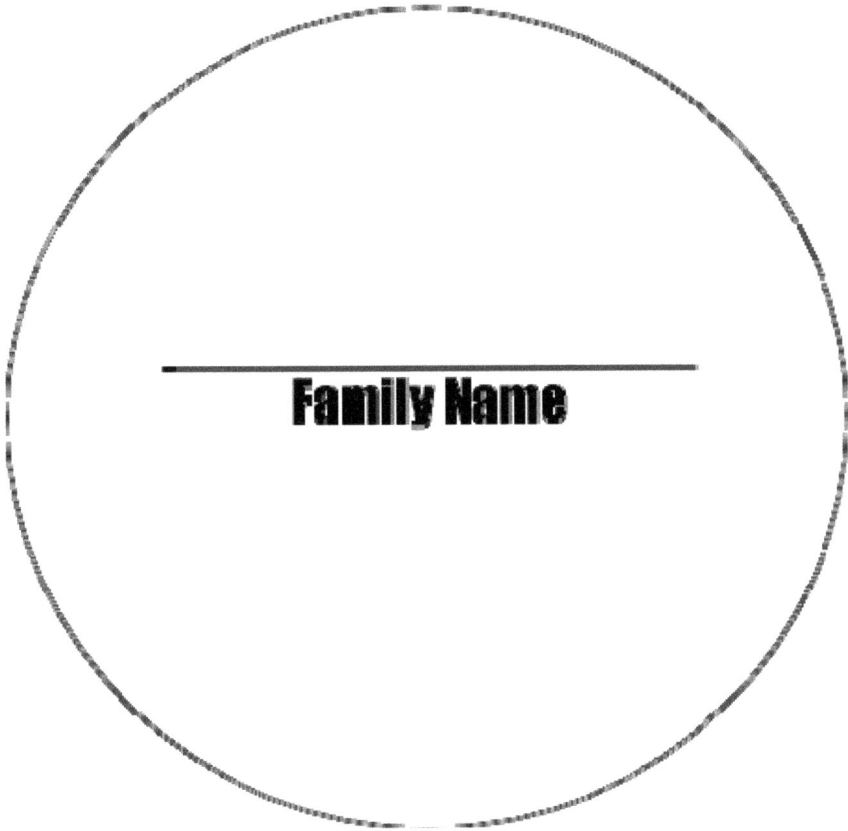

_____

Family Name

The _____ Family Goals:

1. _____

2. _____

3. _____

4. _____

5. _____

About the Author

Robin Marvel is a multi-published author and speaker in the field of self-development. Despite a childhood filled with abuse, homelessness, and teen pregnancy, Robin has overcome many challenges to make her life one of purpose. Today she has devoted her life to show others how to do the same. Using her story, books, and workshops as tools, she is inspiring others to break cycles and choose to live the life they desire.

Guiding you out of struggle and into success, empowering you through sharing her personal journey of struggle, and giving you the tools she used to break out of a victim mindset and into a life of purpose, she walks her talk in all she does!

Working hands-on with Robin Marvel, you will be given life-changing actions paired with effective, easy-to-use daily tools, building a foundation of strength, you will achieve your results. Robin will empower you, encouraging a hands-on approach to your success, holding you accountable to yourself, your actions, and your ultimate success.

You are about to start an adventure that will give you an advantage in your personal and professional life , but you must be ready to step up, keep the ball in your court, and be willing to take action.

Commit to your success with the desire, focus and passion that your life deserves. Robin Marvel will bring you tools, tips, and methods that will produce extraordinary results, enhancing your professional and personal life tenfold!

She invites you to visit her website at www.robinmarvel.com to learn more.

Bibliography

Dyer, W. (2001). *10 secrets for success and inner peace*. Carlsbad, CA: Hay House

Dyer, W. (2006). *Inspiration: Your ultimate calling*. Carlsbad, CA: Hay House

Marvel, R. (2009). *Awakening consciousness A boy's guide!* 1. Ann Arbor, MI: Loving Healing Press

Marvel, R. (2008). *Awakening Consciousness A girl's guide!* 1. Ann Arbor, MI. Loving Healing Press

Paul, A. (2000). *Girlosophy: A Soul Survival Kit*. Crow's Nest, NSW

Ray, V. (1991). *Choosing Happiness: The art of living unconditionally*. New York, NY: Harper Collins Publisher

Ruiz, Don Miguel (2011). *The Fifth Agreement: A practical guide to self mastery*. Amber-allen Publishing (Toltec Wisdom)

Suess. (1990). *Oh, the places you'll go!* New York: Random House. (Children's Book)

Index

A

arrogance, 20

B

bad days, 24
beliefs, 16–18
body image, 12

C

choices, 22
compassion, 28, 42
   forgiveness, 32
convictions, 18–19

D

distractions, 37
domestic violence, 4
drug abuse, 4, 22

E

empty nest, 26–27
energy, personal, 54

F

family
   affirmations, 51
   reflection of you, 2
   roles, 2
family goals, 48–49
forgiveness, 31–34

G

golden rule, 44
gratitude, 35–39

H

homelessness, 4, 22, 61

K

kindness, 41–45

L

love, 57
loving yourself, 5, 11

M

mistakes, 31

N

notecard, 38

P

parenting
   overwhelming, v
patience, 42

peace, 33–34
personal checklist, 6
personal goals, 48
personal responsibility, 21–29
perspective, 12
   and opinions, 19
planning, 50
pregnancy
   teen, vii

R

raise the bar, 55
role model, 10, 12, 23, 24

S

self as a priority, 7
self-care, 5–6
self-image, 11
self-medication, 4
something positive, 53

Journal

_____

_____

_____

_____

_____

_____

_____

_____

_____

_____

_____

_____

_____

_____

_____

_____

_____

_____

_____

7 STEPS TO BALANCE YOUR LIFE!

ROBIN MARVEL

About your life:

- Do you keep asking yourself, when will I be happy?
- Have you forgot what it feels like to be passionate about your life?
- Do you allow excuses to become the reason you are not going after what you desire in your life?
- Do you feel you are worth an amazing life and deserve to get all the things that you desire?
- Have you been following the crowd so long you have lost sight of the real you?

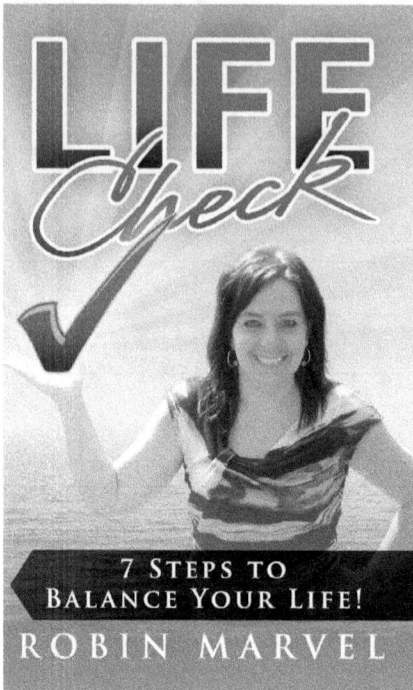

If you answered yes to any of these questions, *Life Check* is the book for you!

Life Check provides simple, effective ways to balance your life. Encouraging you to stop asking what if and start living the life you have imagined. Freeing yourself from the mundane routine of life by providing life tools that will get you rocking the boat, diving in and finding your passion for being alive!

"*Life Check* is the perfect resource for motivation, inspiration, and a reassurance that the life we are looking for is clearly within our reach."

--Victor Schueller, Professor of Positivity and Possibility

"If you are seriously ready to make the changes necessary to create the authentic life you deserve and don't quite know where to begin, I urge you to read and implement the loving guidance contained in this easy to read, straightforward book.

--Rinnell Kelly, Scents of Wellbeing

ISBN 978-1-61599-205-8

We all have a story. Most of our stories have bumps and bruises that leave us at the fork in the road as to where to go next, feeling alone on the journey of life.

Reshaping Reality will encourage you to shake your spirit awake from anything that is limiting you from your potential, propelling you into a life of purpose and meaning, giving you the support needed to grow, evolve, and empower your life. Today, you stop existing and start L-I-V-I-N-G.

Readers who follow the *Reshaping Reality* exercises will:

- Gain tools to reshape programmed beliefs
- Discover what cycles you are stuck in and ways to break them
- Learn how to break patterns of self destruction
- Explore ways to reshape your inner child
- Empower mind, body and spirit by taking an active approach to your life

"Reshaping Reality was very encouraging and spoke directly to me. It has helped me to be aware and let go of my bad habits and programming."   -- Arnbjorg Finnbogadottir

ISBN 978-1-61599-111-2

www.ingramcontent.com/pod-product-compliance
Lightning Source LLC
LaVergne TN
LVHW021135080426
835509LV00010B/1357